Presidents' Day

Aaron Carr

www.av2books.com

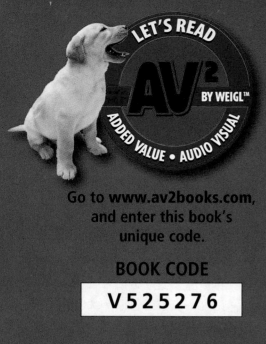

LET'S READ

AV²
BY WEIGL™

ADDED VALUE • AUDIO VISUAL

Go to www.av2books.com, and enter this book's unique code.

BOOK CODE

V 5 2 5 2 7 6

AV² by Weigl brings you media enhanced books that support active learning.

AV² provides enriched content that supplements and complements this book. Weigl's AV² books strive to create inspired learning and engage young minds in a total learning experience.

Your AV² Media Enhanced books come alive with...

Audio
Listen to sections of the book read aloud.

Video
Watch informative video clips.

Embedded Weblinks
Gain additional information for research.

Try This!
Complete activities and hands-on experiments.

Key Words
Study vocabulary, and complete a matching word activity.

Quizzes
Test your knowledge.

Slide Show
View images and captions, and prepare a presentation.

... and much, much more!

Published by AV² by Weigl
350 5th Avenue, 59th Floor New York, NY 10118
Websites: www.av2books.com   www.weigl.com

Library of Congress Control Number: 2014934879

ISBN 978-1-4896-1134-5 (hardcover)
ISBN 978-1-4896-1135-2 (softcover)
ISBN 978-1-4896-1136-9 (single user eBook)
ISBN 978-1-4896-1137-6 (multi-user eBook)

Printed in the United States of America in North Mankato, Minnesota
1 2 3 4 5 6 7 8 9 0 18 17 16 15 14

052014
WEP150314

Project Coordinator: Katie Gillespie   Design and Layout: Ana María Vidal

Weigl acknowledges Getty Images as the primary image supplier for this title.

Let's Celebrate American Holidays

Presidents' Day

CONTENTS

Presidents' Day is celebrated on the third Monday in February. It is a day to honor American presidents.

Presidents' Day began in 1885. The holiday celebrated George Washington's birthday.

George Washington was the first president of the United States.

8

Today, Presidents' Day also honors Abraham Lincoln. He was another famous U.S. president.

In 1968, Lincoln's birthday became a part of Presidents' Day.

Presidents' Day celebrations are held across the country. People read books, watch movies, and sing songs about American presidents.

On Presidents' Day, some people like to visit Washington, D.C. They gather for large celebrations at the Washington Monument and the Lincoln Memorial.

This is a day to learn about American presidents. Special events are held to teach people about Washington and Lincoln.

Presidents' Day is also a time for parades. Many of the floats are colored red, white, and blue.

Red, white, and blue are the colors of the American flag.

Americans honor their presidents in many different ways. Mount Rushmore has carvings of four presidents.

It took 400 people 14 years to carve Mount Rushmore.

Presidents' Day is a time to bring the past to life. People act out famous events from history.

People dress up as Abraham Lincoln or other presidents.

PRESIDENTS' DAY FACTS

These pages provide more detail about the interesting facts found in the book. They are intended to be used by adults as a learning support to help young readers round out their knowledge of each holiday featured in the *Let's Celebrate American Holidays* series.

Pages 4–5

Presidents' Day is celebrated on the third Monday in February. It is officially known as Washington's Birthday, but has become a celebration of all American presidents. It was the first U.S. holiday to honor an individual person. In 1968, people began calling the holiday Presidents' Day.

Pages 6–7

Presidents' Day began in 1885. Washington was born on February 22, 1732. He led the American army in the Revolutionary War against the British and was elected president after the United States became a country. His birthday became an official holiday in Washington, D.C. in 1879. Six years later, it became a holiday for the entire United States.

Pages 8–9

Today, Presidents' Day also honors Abraham Lincoln. Lincoln was born on February 12, 1809. He was elected president in 1861. Like George Washington, he helped people become free. Lincoln held the country together through the Civil War and issued the Emancipation Proclamation to end slavery. Before becoming part of Presidents' Day, his birthday was already a holiday in some states.

Pages 10–11

Special Presidents' Day events are held across the country. Some people like to read history books or watch movies that show presidents giving famous speeches. Though Presidents' Day is a federal holiday, some states celebrate it differently. One of the largest Presidents' Day festivities take place in Laredo, Texas. People celebrate Washington's Birthday with a formal ball, fireworks, parades, and live music.

On Presidents' Day, some people like to visit Washington, D.C. Special events honoring presidents take place at monuments and historic sites. American presidents live and work at the White House. People can take tours to learn more about the history of the building and the presidents.

This is a day to learn about American presidents. Schools have special Presidents' Day lessons and many people read about presidents. George Washington's home in Mount Vernon holds events to teach people about Washington's life. The Lincoln Symposium in Springfield, Illinois, teaches about Lincoln's life and his impact on the country.

Presidents' Day is also a time for parades. Parades often feature floats covered in patriotic red, white, and blue. The parade in Alexandria, Virginia is the largest parade of its kind. It has floats, wagons, horses, bands, youth groups, and historic reenactment groups. Large parades are also held in Philadelphia and Illinois.

Americans honor their presidents in many different ways. The faces of four presidents are carved into Mount Rushmore in the Black Hills of South Dakota. They are George Washington, Thomas Jefferson, Theodore Roosevelt, and Abraham Lincoln. The faces are 60 feet (18 meters) tall and 185 feet (56 m) wide.

Presidents' Day is a time to bring the past to life. Some people like to take part in historical reenactments. People dress in historical clothes and use props to act out famous scenes from history. The Fort Ward Museum in Alexandria, Virginia and the town of Lincoln, Kansas host large reenactment events.

KEY WORDS

Research has shown that as much as 65 percent of all written material published in English is made up of 300 words. These 300 words cannot be taught using pictures or learned by sounding them out. They must be recognized by sight. This book contains 51 common sight words to help young readers improve their reading fluency and comprehension. This book also teaches young readers several important content words, such as proper nouns. These words are paired with pictures to aid in learning and improve understanding.

Page	Sight Words First Appearance
5	a, American, day, in, is, it, on, the, to
6	began, first, of, was
9	also, another, he, part
10	about, and, are, books, country, people, read, songs, watch
13	at, for, large, like, some, they
14	learn, this
17	many, time, white
18	different, four, has, their, took, ways, years
21	as, from, life, or, other, out, up

Page	Content Words First Appearance
5	February, Monday, presidents, Presidents' Day,
6	birthday, holiday, George Washington, United States
9	Abraham Lincoln, today
10	celebrations, movies
13	Lincoln Memorial, Washington, D.C., Washington Monument, White House
14	events
17	blue, colors, flag, floats, parades, red
18	carvings, Mount Rushmore
21	history, past

MEDIA ENHANCED BOOKS
AV²
BY WEIGL™
ADDED VALUE • AUDIO VISUAL

Check out www.av2books.com for activities, videos, audio clips, and more!

The AV² Collection

1 Go to www.av2books.com.

2 Enter book code. V525276

3 Fuel your imagination online!

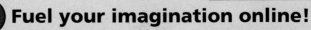

www.av2books.com